My Painting

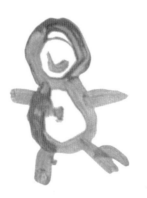

by Sharon Hill

photographs by Kate Handley

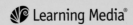 Learning Media®

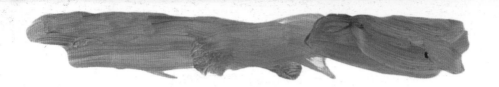

Look at my sky.

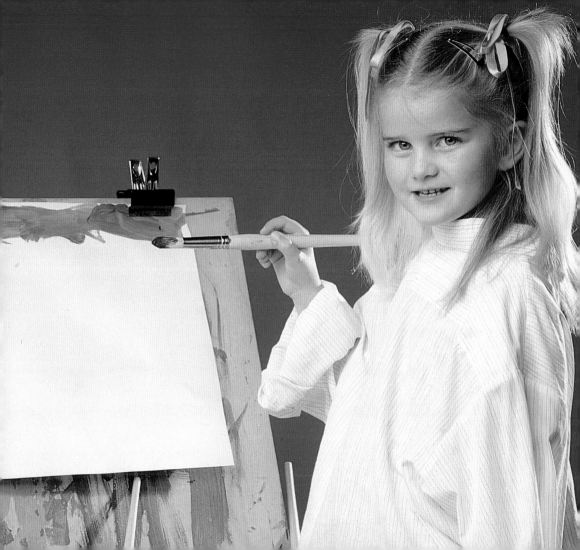

Look at my plane.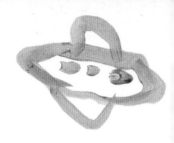

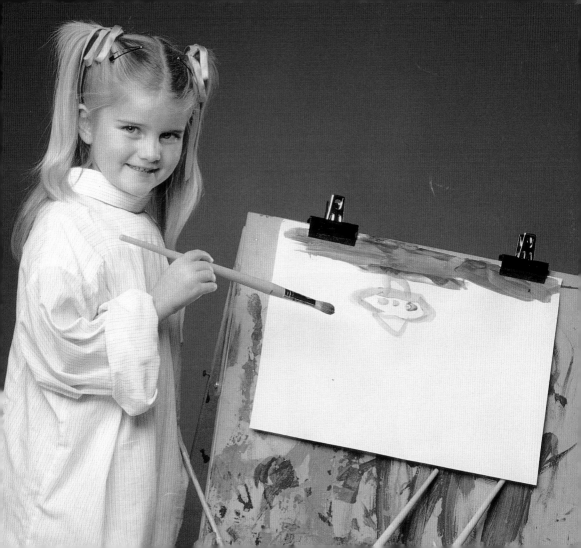

Look at my bridge.

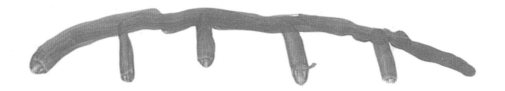

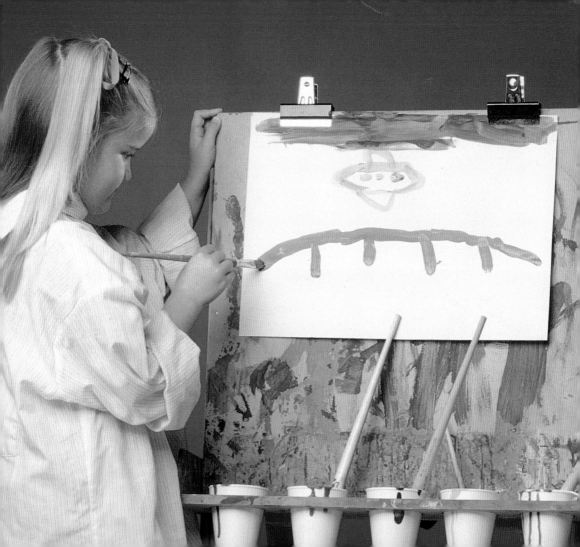

Look at my street.

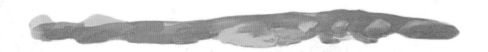

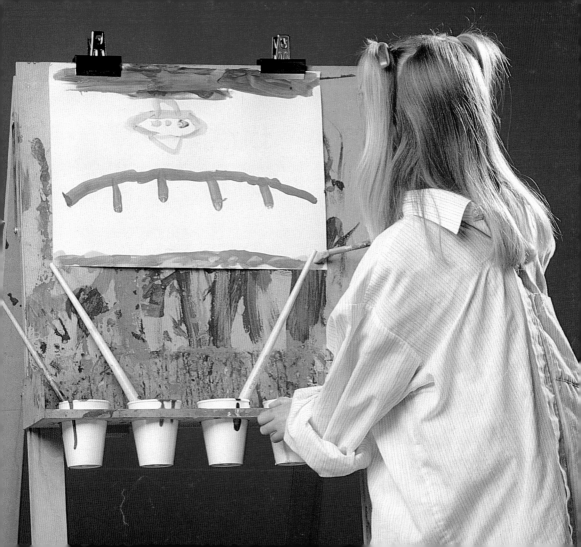

Look at my bus.

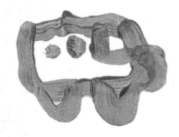

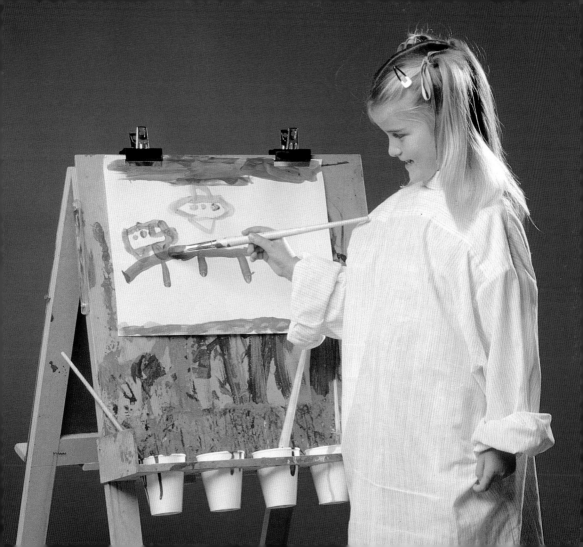

Look at my cab.

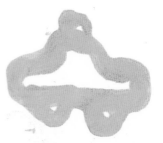

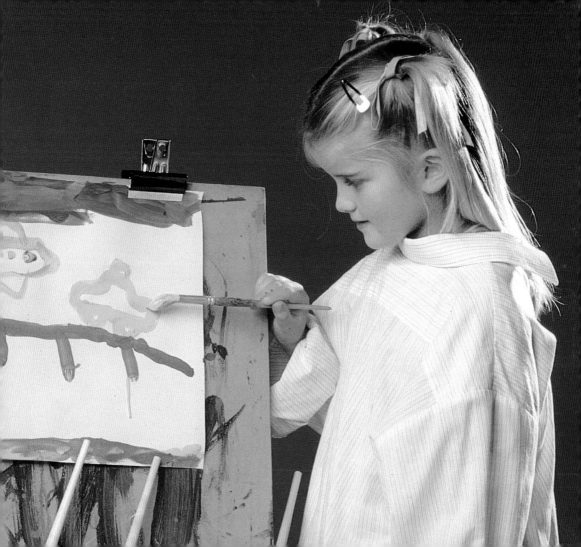

Look at my dog.

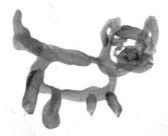

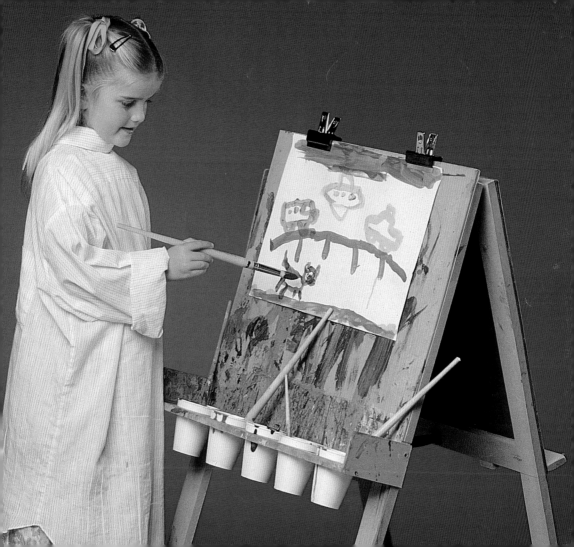

Look at me!

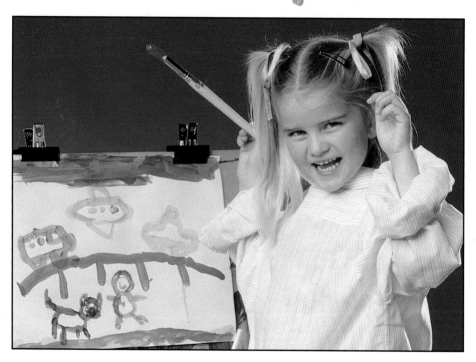